SYSTEM OVER NO TRUMP INTERFERENCE

THE SONTI SOLUTION

Ivan Feit

D1449825

COPYRIGHT

Published by Kindle Direct Publishing/Amazon

1

TABLE OF CONTENTS

2

INTRODUCTION

The evolution of bridge has shown a trend towards preemptive rather than constructive bidding. The 1NT opening bid, which used to discourage opponents from entering the auction, seldom does so today, thereby increasing the need to counter this interference. Unfortunately, there is only one viable convention that has been developed to address this issue. That convention, Lebensohl, is unpopular with the vast majority of duplicate players. I would estimate that fewer than twenty percent of duplicate players use it, and many of them do not understand or utilize it fully. One of the reasons for this is that the system is counter-intuitive and contrary to normal bidding practice. For instance, after an overcall of partner's one notrump opening bid, a direct response of 3NT tells partner that you **don't** have a Stopper in the opponent's suit and **don't** want to play in 3NT, unless partner has one.

More importantly, even when Lebensol is played properly, it is inadequate when it comes to incorporating Transfers, Stayman and other popular bids which are commonly used when there is no interference to our 1NT opening. I used to play Lebensohl, but was dismayed that some of my partners did not. They said it was too difficult to learn and remember. That is what originally motivated me to develop **SONTI**, ___the **acronym** for System Over No Trump Interference.

It took a long time to complete the book because I wanted the material to be comprehensive, yet suitable for players at every level. To that end, the first part of the book is devoted to introducing and demonstrating the use of the two "new" bids that are the foundation of the system. These bids ___ the **"Forcing Two Spade Bid" and the "Translay Double"** are the basic tools of SONTI and can be comprehended and utilized by the majority of newer and aspiring bridge players. Once learned, those players can benefit by utilizing these tools in conjunction with the limited bidding knowledge they possess, and as their skills increase, they can utilize the book fully.

While I advocate the book as an alternative to Lebensohl, (which it is) I do that primarily because many bridge players will know immediately what the subject matter is. However, the text is not a "version" of Lebensohl. It is a completely new and innovative way to view and overcome the obstacles to constructive bidding after the overcall of an opening bid of 1NT. With the exception of a "Comparison of SONTI to Lebensohl" at the end of the book, there is no reference to Lebensohl during the text after this Introduction. Having resolved my concern for having substantive content for the less experienced players by concentrating on the two foundational bids, I turned my attention to creating a comprehensive system for the more experienced players. My goal was to try to utilize every "unused bid" at the two, three and four level, and to cover every type of hand held by the Responder, but it would be necessary to have more tools. Developing them was not too difficult, but as I proceeded down this path it became apparent that with so many tools and so many types of hands, it might be difficult for Responder to decide which bid to make first. That was critical because once Responder got the first bid right, the continuation would be relatively easy, since the SONTI system is very **logical.** The solution was to prioritize the first bid for Responder, so he could quickly identify which priority fit his hand and proceed accordingly.

There are four priorities and I devote a chapter of the text to each one in order of precedence. These chapters deal with overcalls in a natural suit at the 2-level. The fifth chapter deals with overcalls at the 3-level, followed by a sixth chapter which deals with the procedure for coping with Conventional overcalls such as Cappelletti, DON'T, etc. At the conclusion is a "Summary of Feit Responses" (the first bid by Responder and Opener's response to that bid) and a "Comparison of SONTI with Lebensohl." In all, there are 54 hands which are analyzed and 43 "exercise" hands to test your comprehension.

The text includes 9 "new" bids for Responder and 4 more for Opener. It seamlessly incorporates Jacoby and Texas Transfers to all suits, Stayman and/or Puppet Stayman, Stolen Bids, and the Michael's Cue Bid.

I am confident that SONTI will greatly enhance your ability to reach the optimum contract after interference to partner's 1NT opening bid. The new bids are your "tools". More accomplished players will derive greater benefit from them than those with less skill, but everyone can benefit by simply learning the new tools and applying them in conjunction with the bidding skills they currently possess. Once learned, you will look forward to an overcall of your 1NT opening, because you will have a distinct advantage over the competition.

THE SONTI SOLUTION

The Challenge

Everyone loves when their partner opens one notrump. They know that there is a good chance their side has a majority of the high cards. Even beginning players quickly learn how to respond to the one notrump opening. As Responder you learn that you are the one to take control of the auction since partner has made such a descriptive opening bid. By using invitational bids, transfers, Stayman and other conventions, you will usually have little problem guiding your side to the optimum contract. You can find a 4/4, 5/3 or even a 6/2 Major suit fit or play in a Minor suit when necessary. You can find a fit and stop below Game when your side doesn't have quite enough values. It is relatively easy......**except** when the opponents enter the bidding before you, as Responder, have had the opportunity to bid.

The first challenge is that there doesn't seem to be enough space available to bid without getting your side too high. How are you and partner going to show your invitational values, find a Major suit fit, explore for slam, etc.? Unless you have a Game forcing hand, you may be reluctant to enter the bidding at the two or three level, and then you may end up in the wrong contract. And now you have another challenge. **What about the suit the opponents have overcalled?** It will usually be a good suit of five or more cards, and since the opponents have the opening lead, a notrump contract might easily be defeated before you take a single trick. What a dilemma! It's no wonder that no satisfactory system has been devised to solve these problems ... *UNTIL NOW.*

7

The Solution

Part of the solution is to turn a negative into a positive. Instead of lamenting that you do not have enough bidding space, you can take advantage of the fact that your opponents have overcalled. For one thing, they have alerted you to the suit they will probably lead if you persist with a notrump contract. Since you have been forewarned that they may take enough tricks in that suit to set you, you can focus on determining whether your side has a Stopper in that suit. The other good news is that by virtue of their overcall, there are two bids available that you would not otherwise have, namely "double" and a cue bid of Overcaller's suit.

The heart of SONTI is two new bids which I call the **multitaskers**. With so little room to operate, especially at the two level, we must develop bids that can accomplish more than one purpose. This is not a new concept. There are several such bids commonly used in bridge. Here are two examples:

(a) When your partner makes a takeout double, you expect him or her to be short in the bid suit and to have support for the three unbid suits. You dutifully respond in your longest suit, giving preference to a Major as appropriate. When you name your suit, you expect partner will pass or raise that suit since his takeout double implied support for the three unbid suits. However, when partner does not pass or raise your suit but bids their own suit, you come to realize that he has an entirely different type of hand __ one that was too good for an overcall which includes a long and good suit of their own.

(b)When you open 1NT and your partner responds 2♣, the Stayman Convention, you expect him to have a 4-card Major. You dutifully bid a Major if you have one and bid 2♦ if you don't. If you are playing transfers to all four suits, however, Responder may now bid 2NT, showing an invitational no trump raise. This bid, like the previous example shows a completely different type of hand than what you would expect from partner's initial 2♣. He may not have a 4-card Major. The sequence of Responder's 2NT after the initial 2♣ shows an invitational notrump raise. Responder could not invite by bidding 2NT initially because, when playing 4-way transfers, 2NT is a transfer to 3♦.

The two new bids you will be learning shortly, like the examples above, have dual meanings and that is why I call them the **multitaskers**. As the notrump Opener you may be in the dark after partner's initial bid, but don't despair, just make your required response and you will be in the light when partner bids again.

The Multitaskers

The Forcing 2♠ Bid

After an overcall of Opener's 1NT, the bid of 2♠ or the (stolen bid) double of 2♠ by Responder denies a Stopper. Opener's response, in order of precedence, is:

1. *With no Stopper and a 5-card diamond, heart or spade suit, bid three of that suit.*

2. *With a Stopper and a Minimum, bid 2NT and with a Stopper and a Maximum, bid 3NT*

3. *Without a Stopper or a 5-card diamond, heart or spade suit, bid 3♣.*

When Responder bids 2♠ and Opener responds 3♣, they immediately know that neither one has a Stopper and a notrump contract is not advisable.

The Forcing 2♠ bid is also a Multitasker and may be used as a transfer to clubs which Responder will clarify on his next bid.

On the following hands, your partner has opened 1NT with 15-17 high card points and your right-hand opponent has made an Overcall at the 2-level. You are next to bid.

001.　　　♠ K97　♥ QJ6　♦ 985　♣K85

Over any overcall except diamonds, bid 2NT, showing an invitational hand and a Stopper. **Over 2♦,** bid 2♠ showing no Stopper and asking Opener to further describe his hand.

002.　　　♠ K7　♥ Q6　♦ K85　♣K852

Over any overcall except hearts bid 3NT. Over 2♥, bid 2♠ showing no stopper and asking Opener to further describe his hand.

003.　　　♠ J6　♥ A62　♦ Q853　♣KQ93

Over any overcall except spades bid 3NT. Over 2♠, double, stealing the bid, showing no Stopper and asking Opener to further describe his hand.

On the following hands <u>you are the Opener</u> and have opened 1NT. Your left-hand opponent has made an Overcall at the 2 level and your partner, the Responder has bid 2♠ or, if the overcall was 2♠, he has doubled. You are next to bid.

004.   ♠ KJ9   ♥ AQ8   ♦ 985   ♣AK85

If the overcall is any suit except diamonds, bid 3NT showing a Stopper and a Maximum 1NT opening. If the overcall is 2♦, bid 3♣ showing no diamond stopper.

005.   ♠ KJ9   ♥ A98   ♦ 985   ♣AK85

If the overcall is any suit except diamonds, bid 2NT showing a Stopper and a Minimum 1NT opening. If the overcall is 2♦, bid 3♣ showing no diamond stopper.

006.   ♠ KJ985   ♥ A9   ♦ 985   ♣AK8

If the overcall is any suit except diamonds, bid 2NT showing a Stopper and a Minimum 1NT opening. However, if the Overcall is 2♦, bid 3♠ showing no diamond stopper and a 5-card spade suit.

When Responder bids 2♠, he is showing no stopper and if you do not have one, but have a 5-card suit other than clubs, it is prudent for you to bid it because you can be assured of at least a 7-card fit, since partner would not have opened 1NT with a singleton. When you have a Stopper and a 5-card suit, however, it is more important to show your Stopper by bidding either 2NT or 3NT (depending on your strength). You may be able to show your 5-card suit later in the bidding. (stay tuned).

In all of the hands to follow you are you are still the Opener and are responding to partner's forcing 2♠ bid.

007.　　　　♠ KJ9　　♥ 97　♦ KQ852　♣AK8

When the Overcall is 2♥ and Responder bids 2♠, bid 3♦, showing five. Do not worry that partner may have five spades. As you will soon see, partner does not have five spades because in SONTI he would not have bid 2♠ if he did.

008.　　　　♠ 84　　♥ KQJ97　♦ KJ2　♣AJ8

When the overcall is 2♠ and Responder doubles, Opener replies the same way as if Responder had bid 2♠. With the above hand, bid 3♥, showing your 5-card heart suit and no spade Stopper.

009.　　　　♠ 84　　♥ KQJ9　♦ KJ2　♣AJ84

When the overcall is 2♠ and Responder doubles, bid 3♣, showing no stopper and no 5-card diamond, heart or spade suit

010.　　　　♠ 984　　♥ AQ　♦ KJ862　♣AJ8

When the overcall is 2♠ and Responder doubles, bid 3♦ showing five diamonds and no stopper

011.　　　　♠ A84　　♥ Q6　♦ KJ862　♣AJ8

When the overcall is 2♠ and Responder doubles, bid 2NT

The Translay Double

The second of the new bids is the Translay Double. I call it a translay double because it is either a traditional Jacoby transfer or a relay. Opener cannot pass the double and his required response is to bid the next highest suit. Responder will then indicate if the double was a traditional Jacoby transfer, by passing or making the appropriate raise of that suit. If Responder does not pass or raise the suit but proceeds to make any other bid, he has precisely invitational values.

A traditional Jacoby Transfer or Texas Transfer is utilized by Responder, when there is no Overcall of 1NT, to identify a 5-card Major suit and to make the Opener the Declarer in the event that the contract is played in that suit. To implement the Transfer, Responder bids the suit below the suit he wishes the Opener to bid and Opener completes the transfer by bidding the next highest suit. When there is an Overcall, however, the Overcalled suit may be the suit Responder wanted to bid to implement the transfer. In SONTI we solve that problem by doubling that suit. This is known as a "stolen bid". **In SONTI, the "double" of the Overcall is a translay ___either a Traditional Jacoby Transfer or a relay indicating that Responder has precisely invitational values.**

In the following hands you are the Responder, your partner has opened 1NT and there has been an overcall at the 2-level.

010.　　　♠ J84　♥K862　♦ 64　♣AJ86

Over 2♦, make a translay double and follow partner's forced response of 2♥ with 2♠. **Now you are using the Translay Double and Forcing 2♠ bid in combination!** The meaning is logical. Partner should know that your double was not a traditional double because you did not pass or raise hearts. The double was a relay showing precisely invitational values ___not invitational or better. The 2♠ bid shows no stopper and is asking you to further describe your hand. As the bidding continues you must keep in mind that you are in an invitational, not Game-forcing auction.

011.　　　♠ J84　♥K862　♦AJ64　♣86

Over 2♣, double and follow the 2♦ forced bid with 2♠ as before showing and invitational hand and no Stopper.

012.　　　♠ J84　♥62　♦AJ64　♣K986

Over 2♥, you cannot show your invitational values because a double of 2♥ will elicit 2♠ from partner and you can't physically make the forcing bid 2♠ when your partner bid that suit. You could try to double your partner's 2♠ bid but I don't think your opponents would let you do that. You can't start with a Translay double but must bid 2♠ directly and partner will not know if you have Game forcing or invitational values. The partnership should keep that in mind as the bidding progresses

013.　　　♠ A84　♥A62　♦643　♣K986

Over 2♦, bid 2♠. Partner will know you have Game going values! How does he know? ....

This is an important aspect of SONTI. It is what I call a "Negative Implication." He knows that if you had invitational values, you would have doubled to relay to hearts and then bid 2♠ to show invitational values. Since you bid 2♠ directly, he knows that you have Game going values.

16

Combining the Old with the New

After you have learned the new bids you may feel like a child with a new toy. The old bids, however, the ones you are currently using as Responder when there is no interference, are still valuable, indispensable and interact beautifully with the new bids. Let's take a look at the some of the most useful bids which are not available to you in Lebensohl, but fit seamlessly in SONTI.

(a) Jacoby and Texas Transfers

Jacoby and Texas Transfers in SONTI work the same way as when there is no overcall. Responder bids the suit below the one he wants Opener to bid (assuming it is available) and Opener complies by bidding it, thereby assuring that Opener with the stronger hand becomes the Declarer.

(b) The Stayman Convention

The bid of 3♣ by Responder is Stayman or Puppet Stayman. Either will work well with SONTI. Playing regular Stayman, the responses are the same except that they are at the three level. If Opener has a 4-card major suit, he bids it and if he does not, he bids 3♦.

The primary benefit of Puppet Stayman is the ability for Opener to show a five-card Major suit. If you and partner customarily play Puppet Stayman over 2NT or 1NT, I suggest you play it here. If not, and you don't want to learn Puppet Stayman, standard Stayman over any overcall will be adequate. If the overcall is in a Major suit, Stayman or Puppet Stayman is inquiring about the other Major. You don't want to play in the suit of the Overcaller.

(c) Stolen Bids:

This simple and very useful convention (sometimes called "mirror bids") works seamlessly over notrump interference since it **takes up no bidding space**. If the overcall is the suit you would have bid if there were no overcall, simply double the overcall and partner will respond as if you were the one making that bid. For instance, if the overcall is 2♦ and **you** wanted to bid 2♦ to make a transfer bid to hearts simply "steal" that bid by doubling and partner will complete the transfer to hearts. If the overcall is 2♥, and you want to make a transfer to spades just double and partner will similarly complete the transfer to 2♠. **If the overcall is 2♠ and you want to use the forcing 2♠, "steal" that bid with a "double", and Opener will respond as if you had bid 2♠ directly.**

(d) The Cue Bid

When our opponents make an overcall, they afford us two additional bids ... "double" and the cue bid (bid or their suit). In SONTI we utilize cue bids for a variety of purposes. Examples will follow.

SONTI IN ACTION

We are now ready to begin the journey to Sontiland. We will cross quickly over the Lebensohl Valley, scale the Cappelletti Mountains, go through Interference Pass, and befriend the natural suited, artificial suited and two suited tribes. Yes, we will overcome everything in our path to reach the Promised Land. Be sure to pack smartly for the trip, bringing along everything you know about bidding after your partner opens 1NT. I will furnish you with several more tools as we go along the way such as the "Partial Stopper Cue bid", the "Scrambling 3NT" and the "Feit Invite", so sit back, relax and enjoy the trip.

The SONTI System can be used with any opening one notrump point range. Indeed, it will be even more useful to partners opening a weak notrump (including those playing ACOL or Precision) as overcalls will be more frequent. *For all of the examples which follow, however, it will be assumed that partner has opened with 15 to 17 high card points.* Partnerships can simply adjust their bidding accordingly when opening with other ranges. It is also assumed that your partnership will frequently open 1NT with a 5-card Major suit, which is becoming a more common practice.

All references to a "Stopper" pertain to a holding that will stop the running of the suit bid by the Overcaller. In examples 001 to 030 to follow, partner has opened 1NT and your right-hand opponent has made an overcall in a <u>natural suit</u> at the 2 level. We will discuss countering overcalls at the 3- level, and conventional overcalls in one and two suited hands in later segments.

WHO ARE YOU?

Yes, I know you know who you are but I want to clarify that when I refer to "you" in the examples to follow, you know that your role is always the same. "You" are the third person to bid. after your partner has opened 1NT and your right-hand opponent (RHO) has made an overcall. I will refer to your partner as the Opener or your partner, (who has bid 1NT.) I will always refer to your RHO, the second to bid, as the Overcaller.

SONTI After a 2♣ Overcall

After a 2♣ overcall of 1NT, it is common practice to use "double" by Responder as a "stolen bid" to designate Stayman with "all systems on". The assumption is that the overcall is hindering our communication and we can compensate by "stealing" the 2♣ Stayman bid with a double. With SONTI, however, we welcome the "interfering" 2♣ bid because it warns us of the "dangerous" club suit and allows lots of bidding space, wherein we can implement our new bids to determine if we have a club Stopper, an invitational hand, and whether we have a Major suit fit. Moreover, we can sometimes utilize a translay double of 2♣ as a transfer to 2♦ wherein a diamond contract, played by Opener, might be our best spot.

It is important to not panic when your partner's one notrump opening is overcalled. Be happy that you have been overcalled because you know which suit needs to be "stopped" and you automatically have two tools with which to work that you would not have if your right-hand opponent (RHO) had passed __namely "double" and a cue bid. Moreover, you have the new SONTI bids, described above, in addition to the bids you were using before, including Transfers, and Stayman. Keep in mind that you are now "in control" and there is much you want to accomplish. You may want to reach a part score contract, invite or force partner to Game or Slam, find a 4/4 or 5/3 or 6/2 fit in a Major, play in a Minor suit or play in a notrump contract, after making sure your partnership has a Stopper in the Overcaller's suit. Also, you will want your partner to be the Declarer so that the lead will come up to him. So much to think about and so many choices! But relax because I am going to **prioritize** for you:

When reading the analysis of each hand, if you are uncertain about the meaning of the initial bid by Responder or the initial rebid by the 1NT Opener, refer to the "Summary of Feit Responses" on pages 69-72.

CHAPTER I

Priority # 1

No Stopper and a 5-Card or Longer Major Suit

014. ♠ Q9843 ♥ 8 ♦ 9764 ♣ J97

If RHO had passed you would have bid 2♥ to transfer to spades to "protect" partner from having to play this hand at 1NT. When partner bid 2♠ you would pass, but prospects would likely be bleak. Now that RHO has bid, you are off the hook and should pass.

015. ♠ KQJ86 ♥ 86 ♦ 962 ♣ 973

Over 2♣ or 2♦ make a traditional (Jacoby) transfer bid of 2♥ and over 2♥ double, to transfer to 2♠ and pass.

016. ♠ KQ9862 ♥ J8 ♦2 ♣ KJ3

After any overcall bid 4♥ to transfer to 4♠ and pass. This is a traditional Texas Transfer.

017. ♠763 ♥ AQ10863 ♦ K2 ♣ K4

After any overcall bid 4♦ to transfer to 4♥ and pass.

In an effort to keep SONTI as simple as possible I have endeavored to make very few changes in the way conventions such as Transfers are used. After an overcall, however, we need to consider not only if we have an 8-card fit and sufficient values for Game, but whether we have a Stopper. Therefore, we are going to make a slight modification to the invitational bids. In considering a **rhyming** name for this bid I immodestly decided on the **"Feit Invite"** which is described below:

The Feit Invite

After an overcall of 1NT and subsequent transfer or translay double to a Major, Responder, with invitational values, has two choices to invite Game. <u>When Responder has a Stopper, he invites with 2NT and without a Stopper he invites with 3 of the Major.</u> When Responder invites with 2NT (showing a Stopper) and Opener has a Minimum and 2-card support, he passes, but with 2card support and a Maximum, he raises 2NT to 3NT. When Responder invites with 2NT and Opener has a Minimum and 3-card support, he bids three of the Major which Responder passes, but with 3-card support and a Maximum he bids four of the Major. With 4-card or more support and either a Minimum or Maximum, he raises to four of the Major.

When Responder invites with three of the Major, Showing no Stopper and Opener has two or 3-card Support and a Minimum, he passes, even if he has a Stopper. When Opener has 2-card support, a Maximum and a Stopper, he bids 3NT and with a Maximum and 3-card support, he bids four of the Major. With 4-card or more support and a Minimum or a Maximum, Opener raises three of the Major to four of the Major.

018.   ♠A4   ♥ QJ862   ♦KJ6   ♣ QJ9

Over 2♣, bid 2♦ and **over 2♦** double, to transfer to hearts. Then bid 3NT. Opener passes with two hearts and bids 4♥ with three or more. In this case it appears that you made a translay double with more than invitational values. This is not inconsistent with the system, however, as the 3NT bid by you is, in essence, a heart raise which confirmed that the double was a transfer rather than an indication of invitational values.

Over 2♠, bid 3♦ to transfer to hearts and then bid 3NT. With only two hearts partner will pass and with three he will bid 4♥.

As will be shown later when Minor suits are discussed, 3♦ normally shows a weak hand with long diamonds. Over a spade overcall, however, 3♦ is a transfer to hearts.

019.   KJ864   ♥ Q107   ♦98   ♣ K85

Over 2♦, bid 2♥ to transfer to 2♠ and follow with an invitation of 3♠. This sequence confirms five or more spades, an invitational hand and no Stopper. With a Minimum, partner passes (unless he has four or more spades) and with a Maximum and three or more spades, he bids 4♠. If Opener has two spades, a Maximum and a Stopper, he bids 3NT and with a Minimum, two spades and no Stopper he passes.

Over 2♣ or 2♥, Responder bids 2NT showing an invitational hand and a Stopper. If Opener has a Minimum he passes, but with a Maximum and at least three spades, he raises to 3NT.

Exercise on Priority #1

* See answers below

1. ♠ A8765   ♥ K96   ♦ A5   ♣ J106

Opener	Overcaller	Responder	Advancer
1NT	2♦	?	

2. ♠ KQ765   ♥ K96   ♦5   ♣ Q1064

Opener	Overcaller	Responder	Advancer	1
1NT	2♥	?		

3. ♠ A87   ♥ KQ642   ♦75   ♣Q106

Opener	Overcaller	Responder	Advancer
1NT	2♠	?	

4. ♠ 876   ♥ J9642   ♦ 95   ♣ J1065

Opener	Overcaller	Responder	Advancer
1NT	2♣	?	

5. ♠ A8   ♥ KQJ96   ♦ Q642   ♣ J10

Opener	Overcaller	Responder	Advancer
1NT	2♦	?	

6. ♠ A8765   ♥ K96   ♦ 95   ♣Q954

Opener	Overcaller	Responder	Advancer
1NT	2♦	2♥	pass
2♠	pass	?	

7. ♠ A8765   ♥ K6   ♦ KJ7   ♣Q106

Opener	Overcaller	Responder	Advancer
1NT	2♥	dbl	pass
2♠	pass	?	

08.	♠ KQ873	♥ 854	♦ J7	♣ QJ86

Opener	Overcaller	Responder	Advancer
1NT	2♣	2♥	pass
2♠	pass	?	

09.	♠ AKQ6432	♥ KQ8	♦7	♣ A4

Opener	Overcaller	Responder	Advancer
1NT	2♦	4♥	pass
4♠	pass	?	

* Answers to Exercise on Priority #1

1. Two hearts
2. Double, translay
3. Three diamonds
4. Pass
5. Double, translay
6. Three spades, invitation without stopper
7. Three notrump, requests Opener to pass with 2 spades and correct to 4 spades with three or more
8. Two notrump, five spades, invitation with stopper
9. Four notrump

Three Clubs

The bid of 3♣ is a Game forcing form of the Stayman Convention. One of the advantages of the 3♣ bid is that it is available over any 2-level overcall. It is forcing to 3NT or four of a Minor and guarantees a Stopper or a distributional hand that is unsuitable for play in notrump. It should be easy to remember the 3♣ Stayman bid because it is similar to the 2♣ Stayman bid. If the overcall is in hearts, 3♣ is inquiring about spades and if the overcall is in spades, it is inquiring about hearts. You don't want to be playing in the opponent's suit.

The response to 3♣ is the same as the response to the 2♣ Stayman bid, when there was no overcall, except that your bids will be at the three level rather than the two level. You bid three of your Major if you have one, and 3♦ if you do not. If you do not have a Major suit fit, you can safely fall back to 3NT because the *3C* bid guarantees a Stopper or a distributional hand with "extra" values that are needed to play at the four level or above.

The 3♣ bid can be used directly after the overcall or indirectly after Opener's response of 2NT to the forcing 2♠ bid. Of course, Responder can't bid 3♣ if the Opener responds 3♣ to the 2♠ bid. In that case, we will search for a Major suit fit by bidding "up the line".

Two More New Bids

The Partial Stopper Cue Bid

After Opener responds 3♣ to your 2♠, the partnership will proceed to bid "up the line" to find the best contract. In doing so, we use a cue bid (bid of opponent's suit) to show a partial Stopper in the Overcaller's suit. A partial Stopper is a holding of Qx, Jxx or 109xx. If partner also holds Qx, Jxx or 109xx, the partnership will be able to stop the running of that suit.

The Scrambling 3NT

When it becomes apparent that neither Opener or Responder has a Stopper and either one bids 3NT, it is not "to play". The partnership will then proceed to bid 4-card suits "up the line" until at least a 4/3 fit is found.

At this point I want to emphasize that it is not necessary to memorize bidding sequences even though I detail them in the example hands. If you learn the three basic "tools" which are the translay double, the forcing 2♠ bid and the 3♣ Bid, and apply them with common sense and the bidding skills you already have, you will do well. When in doubt do what is logical.

CHAPTER II

Priority # 2

Four Card Major Suits

020.   ♠ A J9   ♥ K963   ♦ A5   ♣ J1032

After any overcall, bid 3♣ as Stayman. (You have Stoppers in every suit). **This bid is forcing to 3NT or 4 of a Minor and guarantees a Stopper or a hand that is unsuitable for notrump.** If partner bids 3♥, bid four. If he bids 3NT, pass and if he bids 3♦, bid 3NT.

On the above hand, Responder had Game going values and Stoppers. We are now going to take a look at some hands with a 4-card Major and no Stopper.

021. ♠KJ74 ♥6 ♦KJ75 ♣A985

Over 2♥, bid 2♠. If partner shows a Stopper by bidding 2NT, bid 3♣ as Stayman for spades. If he bids 3♠, bid four. If he bids 3♦ after your 3♣, bid 3NT (his 2NT guaranteed a Stopper). If he bids 3NT, pass.

If partner bids 3♣ denying a Stopper, bid 3♦ (up the line). If he bids 3♥, he is showing a partial heart Stopper and, since you don't have one, bid 3♠. If partner bids 3♠, raise to four. If he bids 3NT, (**Scrambling Notrump),** bid 4♣.

022. ♠9 ♥Q853 ♦KQ86 ♣AJ74

Over 2♠, double (stolen bid). If partner bids 2NT bid 3♣ as Stayman (for hearts) and if he bids 3NT, pass. If partner bids 3♥ (showing five), raise to four. If he bids 3♦ (showing five) raise to 5♦.

If partner responds 3♣ to your 2♠, start with 3♦. This bid is forcing because partner didn't have the opportunity to make a translay double to show invitational values. If partner bids 4♦, showing four, raise to five. (He doesn't have the ace or king of spades so all of his high cards will be working). If he bids 3♥ (showing four), raise to four and if he bids 3♠, he will be showing a partial Stopper and since you don't have one, bid 4♣.

023. ♠ KJ95 ♥ Q853 ♦ K98 ♣ A8

Over 2♠, bid 3♣ as Stayman showing a spade Stopper and Game going hand. If partner bids 3♥, raise to four and if he bids 3♦ denying hearts, bid 3NT.

024. ♠ J75 ♥ KJ92 ♦ 82 ♣ A943

Over 2♦, double to show your invitational values and follow 2♥ with 2♠ to ask for a Stopper. If Opener bids 2NT showing a Stopper and a Minimum, pass. If he bids 3♥ or 3♠, he will be showing five of that suit and you will raise to four.

If partner bids 3♣ in response to your 2♠ showing no diamond Stopper, you need to shift to defensive mode.
3NT is not an option since neither you or partner have a diamond Stopper. This is the ***worst- case scenario...... no Stopper and uncertain whether you have enough points for Game.*** Partner may have a Maximum, however, and he could have four hearts.

The procedure in this situation is for you and partner to bid "up the line" to show 4-card suits, hoping to find a playable 4/3 fit or perhaps a 4/4 fit. Therefore, after 3♣ show your 4-card heart suit by bidding 3♥. Opener will know that you have exactly four hearts because you did not make a heart raise after his initial 2♥ call. He will also know that you have only invitational values because of your initial double. If partner has four hearts and a Minimum, he will likely pass and with four hearts and a Maximum, he will raise to four. With only three hearts and a Minimum or Maximum he should pass. He could gamble that you have four spades as well as four hearts but the odds are against it. He should be content that, without a Stopper and your limited values, you have found a playable contract. If Opener has only two hearts and four spades, he will bid 3♠ which you will pass. If he has only two hearts and three spades, he will bid 4♣ which you will pass.

Observe that with only five cards in the Majors, Opener must have eight cards in the Minors, so it is almost certain that he has at least four clubs. Even if he has five diamonds and three clubs, it would be better to play in clubs than diamonds since Responder likely has five diamonds.

Take note that Opener knows you do not have five hearts or five spades because your initial bid would have been a translay double or 2♥ transfer bid, followed by a pass or raise of that suit if you did (Priority #1), and you knew that he did not have five hearts or five spades because, with no Stopper and a five card Major, he would have bid three of that Major instead of 3♣.

When Responder doubles 2♦, or 2♥ and does not pass or raise Opener's heart or spade response [2NT and 3NT are a raise], and makes another bid, his double is a Translay, not a Transfer, denoting a hand with invitational values__ not forcing to Game.

When Responder has "room" to double to show invitational values, but does not, his subsequent bids are forcing to 3NT or four of a Minor.

Puppet Stayman

Puppet Stayman is commonly played after partner opens 2NT, but it can be played over 1NT as well. After partner's opening 1NT or 2NT, Responder bids three clubs and when Opener has a five-card Major, he bids three of that Major. When Opener has a 4-card Major, he bids three diamonds. If Responder has a 4-card Major, he bids three of the Major he <u>doesn't</u> have. If Opener's Major is the one Responder bid, he bids 3NT, because Responder doesn't have that Major, he has the other one. If Opener's Major is the Major that Responder didn't bid, then they have a fit and they proceed to play in that suit. The benefit of this Convention. in addition to the ability to find the 5/3 fit is that Opener, with the stronger hand becomes the Declarer.

In SONTI, Opener can show his 5-card suit in response to Responder's forcing 2♠, but only if he doesn't have a Stopper. When he has a Stopper and a 5-card suit, he bids 2NT with a Minimum and 3NT with a Maximum. If you are playing Puppet Stayman, after the 2♠/2NT sequence, Responder can bid 3♣ as Puppet Stayman and Opener can show the 5-card Major that he was unable to show at his first turn. After the 2♠/3NT sequence, however, there is no way for Opener to identify a 5-card Major as it would be foolish to risk looking for a 5/3 Major fit at the 4-level when you already are in a playable 3NT contract. When Responder bids 3♣ directly after the overcall, it is even more beneficial to be playing Puppet Stayman. It is not necessary to play Puppet Stayman in SONTI, as regular Stayman is sufficient more often than not. However, there are some hands where Puppet Stayman is the only way to find a 5/3 Major suit fit.

The following three hands will demonstrate the benefits of playing Puppet Stayman in SONTI.

025.   ♠ AJ6   ♥ Q982   ♦ A643   ♣ Q8

Over 2♦, if you are playing regular Stayman, bid 3♣ and, if Opener does not have a four or five card Major, he will bid 3NT since your 3♣ promises a Stopper. If partner bids 3♥, you will bid four but if he bids 3♠, you won't know if he has four or five. You will assume that he has four (much more likely) and bid 3NT, thereby missing the 5/3 fit. If you are playing Puppet, Opener will be able to show his 5-card spade suit in response to your 3♣, enabling you to reach the optimum 4♠.

026.   ♠QJ6   ♥KQ8   ♦K6   ♣ Q8642

Over 2D, bid 3NT. If you are playing Puppet Stayman, however, bid 3♣ and if partner has a 5-card Major, he will bid it and you will raise to four, which would likely be your best contract. If he does not show a 5-card major, bid 3NT.

027.   ♠A86   ♥Q987   ♦42   ♣ KQ86

Over 2♦, if you are playing Puppet Stayman, start with 2♠. If partner bids 3NT, pass but if he bids 2NT showing a Stopper, bid 3♣. If he has a 5-card Major, he will bid it and you will raise to four. If he bids 3♦ showing one or both 4-card Majors, bid 3♠ **indicating four hearts**.

If his suit is hearts, he will bid 4♥. If his suit is spades, he will bid 3NT which you will pass. Take note that your 3♣, after partner's 2NT, was forcing to Game since, in effect, it was an acceptance of an invitation and forcing because you could have passed 2NT.

Exercise on Priority #2

1.

♠ K87	♥ KQ85	♦ 8642	♣ A8
Opener	Overcaller	Responder	Advancer
1NT	2♠	?	

2.

♠ K87	♥ KQ85	♦ 64	♣ KJ86
Opener	Overcaller	Responder	Advancer
1NT	2♦	2♠	pass
2NT	pass	?	

3.

♠ 874	♥ Q85	♦ K864	♣ AJ5
Opener	Overcaller	Responder	Advancer
1NT	2♠	dbl	pass `
3♦	pass	?	

4.

♠ AQ87	♥ KQ5	♦ 64	♣ AQ97
Opener	Overcaller	Responder	Advancer
1NT	2♦	2♠	pass
2NT	pass	3♣	pass
3♠	pass	?	

5.

♠ J87	♥ AJ54	♦ 642	♣ K98
Opener	Overcaller	Responder	Advancer `
1NT	2♦	dbl	pass
2♥	pass	2♠*	pass
2NT	pass	?	

6.

♠ Q83	♥ AQ53	♦ 64	♣ K986
Opener	Overcaller	Responder	Advancer
1NT	2♦	2♠	pass
3♣	pass	?	

36

Answers to Exercise on Priority #2

1. Three clubs, direct Stayman
2. Three clubs, indirect Stayman
3. Pass, no Stopper
4. Four spades, no diamond Stopper
5. Pass, 2NT shows invitational values and a Stopper
6. Three hearts

Negative Implications

One bidding skill that more experienced players have developed and lesser players should be working on, is the use of negative implications. The former will derive more benefit from SONTI than the latter, but do not despair if you are less skilled in this regard. You can gain great benefit from SONTI as long as you **learn the new tools and utilize them in accordance with common sense and the bidding skills you currently possess.** Here are some examples of negative implications, for both Opener and Responder, that are available in SONTI:

1. When **Responder's** first bid is **not** a transfer or translay double, he doesn't have a 5-card Major, because transferring to a Major would have been his first priority.

2. When **Responder** bypasses 2♠ and bids 3♣, he has a Stopper or is not worried about one because he has a distributional hand that is unsuitable for play in notrump.

3. When **Opener** responds 3♣ to 2♠ or the stolen bid double of 2♠, he does not have five diamonds, five hearts or five spades.

4. When **Opener** responds 3♣ to 2♠ and either partner subsequently bids 3NT, it is not "to play" because neither partner has a Stopper.

5. When the overcall is in a Major suit, Stayman or Puppet Stayman is inquiring about the other Major, since you don't want to play in Overcaller's suit.

6. When either partner skips a suit at the three level in the "up the line" procedure, he has less than four cards in that suit.

7. When **Opener** bids a suit at the three level in the "up the line" procedure, he has exactly four cards in that suit. With five he would have bid three of that suit directly over 2♠.

8. When Opener responds 3♣ to 2♠, he does not have the ace or king in the overcalled suit.

9. When partner responds 3♦, 3♥ or 3♠ to the 2♠ bid, showing five, he likely does not have another 4-card suit, since his "even" distribution should be 5332.

10. When Responder bypasses **the opportunity** to make a translay double to show invitational values and bids 2♠ directly, he has better than invitational values and his bid is forcing to Game or four of a Minor.

CHAPTER III

Priority #3

No Four or Five Card Major Suit

029. ♠ K87 ♥ Q105 ♦ K85 ♣ J1094

After any overcall bid 2NT. This natural and logical bid shows an invitational hand with a Stopper in every suit.

030. ♠ K73 ♥ K52 ♦ 84 ♣ K8653

After any overcall except diamonds, bid 2NT showing an invitational hand with a Stopper. If partner bids 3NT, pass. **Over 2♦** start with a double and follow the forced 2♥ response with 2♠. **This sequence shows an invitational hand with no five-card Major and no Stopper. If he had better than an invitational hand, partner would have bid 2♠ directly and your side would be forced to Game or four of a Minor.** If partner bids 2NT or 3NT, pass. If partner bids 3♥ or 3♠ showing five, bid four. If partner bids 3♣, pass.

031. ♠ K73 ♥ K52 ♦ A4 ♣ K8653

This is the same hand except we have a diamond Stopper. Now, over 2♦, bid 3NT.

032. ♠ KJ6 ♥ 97 ♦ KJ97 ♣ A865

Over 2H, bid 2S. If partner bids 2NT, bid 3NT. If he bids 3♠, bid four. If Opener responds 3♣ to your 2♠, bid 3♦ and if he bids 3♠ (showing 4), bid 4♠. You know he doesn't have five spades because, without a Stopper, he would have responded 3♠ to your 2♠ rather than 3♣. The 4/3 fit may be problematic, but 4♠ should be a good contract considering that most of partner's high card points will be "working". (He doesn't have the ace or king of hearts). If he bids 3NT(Scrambling), bid 4♣.

033. ♠ K87   ♥ Q5   ♦ K85   ♣ KJ95

Over 2♥ bid 2♠ and follow 2NT with 3NT. If Opener bids 3♣, bid 3♥. This sequence denotes a partial Stopper in hearts. **(Partial Stopper Cue bid).** If partner has Jxx, or 109xx in hearts, he will know that the heart suit can be stopped and will bid 3NT. If he does not have a partial Stopper and continues the "up the line" sequence with 3♠ you have four choices. You can either pass, bid a scrambling 3NT, bid 4♠ or 4♣. **What would you do?**

Since partner did not bid 3♠ over your 2♠, you know he only has four spades. If you play in spades you will have a 4/3 fit and in clubs you will likely have a 4/4 or 5/4 fit, but will need an extra trick. The key to the hand is that your heart queen is likely worthless.

Partner does not have the ace or king of hearts because he would have bid 2NT or 3NT instead of 3♣ if he had either of those cards. Also, he probably does not have the heart jack, because with Jxx he would have had the matching partial Stopper you needed to play in 3NT. This hand is a great example of "**negative implications**". Taking everything into consideration, the best action is to pass 3♠.

034. ♠ K96   ♥ K96   ♦ Q7   ♣ A8532

Over 2♣, 2♥ or **2♠** bid 3NT. **Over 2♦** bid 2♠ and if partner bids 3♥ or 3♠ showing five, raise to four. If he bids 3♣, bid 3♦ showing a partial Stopper and, if he has one too, he will bid 3NT. If he bids 3NT which is the Scrambling 3NT, bid 4♣. If he bids 4♣, pass since the diamond queen will be worthless.

035.   ♠ J109   ♥ Q8   ♦ QJ84   ♣ K873

Over 2♣ or 2♦, bid 2NT which guarantees a Stopper, invitational values and a balanced hand. This bid denies a 5-card Major suit since you would have doubled 2♦ if you had five hearts (stolen bid) or bid 2♥ (transfer) if you had five spades. If partner has a Minimum opening, he will pass your 2NT invitation.

If he has a Maximum and a 5-card Major he will bid three of the Major. **That bid is an acceptance of your invitation and is forcing to Game.** With the above hand you will raise 3♠ to four and will bid 3NT over 3♥. If partner has a Maximum but no 5-card Major, he will bid 3NT. Otherwise he will pass 2NT.

Over 2♥, bid 2♠. If partner bids 2NT or 3NT pass. If partner bids 3♦ showing five, pass. (He "should" not have a 4 or 5-card Major.) If partner bids 3♣, bid 3♥ showing a partial Stopper. If partner follows with 3NT, that will confirm that he has a partial Stopper too and you will pass. If partner does not have a partial Stopper and bids 3S you should pass to play in the 4/3 fit. You know he has exactly four spades because he would have bid 3♠ over your 2♠ if he had five.

036.   ♠ K87   ♥ Q6   ♦ AJ7   ♣ A985

After any overcall **except 2♥,** if you are playing regular Stayman, bid 3NT. If you are playing Puppet Stayman, bid 3♣ and if partner bids 3♠, showing five, bid four. Otherwise, bid 3NT. **Over 2H,** start with 2♠ and pass partner's 3NT or raise 2NT to three. If partner bids 3♠, raise to four.

If **partner bids 3♣** over 2♠, bid 3♥ to show a partial Stopper and he will bid 3NT if he has one. If he bids 3♠, you know that he has exactly four spades because his 3♣ denied five, but raise

4.

to 4♠ anyway to play in the 4/3 fit. Your "extra" high card points should compensate for the lack of an eight-card fit. If he bids 3NT (Scrambling), bid 4♣.

037.   ♠Q5   ♥A6   ♦QJ76   ♣K9732

Over 2♣, 2♦ or 2♥, bid 3NT. **Over 2S** start with a double (stolen bid). If partner bids 2NT, bid 3NT. If he bids **3♣**, bid 3♦ (up the line); if he next bids 3♥, bid 3♠, the partial Stopper cue bid. If he bids 3NT confirming a partial Stopper, pass. If he bids 4♣, pass. Your spade queen will be worthless as partner does not have the ace or king.

When either partner bids 3NT after a partial Stopper cue bid, it is "to play" not Scrambling even though both partners have previously shown "no Stopper".

Exercise on Priority #3

1.

♠ K87	♥ AJ5	♦ 64	♣ Q986
Opener	Overcaller	Responder	Advancer
1NT	2♦	2♠	pass
3♣	pass	?	

2.

♠ 86	♥ KQ8	♦ KQ9	♣ AK86
Opener	Overcaller	Responder	Advancer
1NT	2♠	dbl	pass
3♥	pass	?	

3.

♠ A87	♥ KQ8	♦ KQJ7	♣ 865
Opener	Overcaller	Responder	Advancer
1NT	2♣	2♦	pass
2♥	pass	3♥	pass
?			

4.

♠ AQ7	♥ KQ8	♦ KQJ7	♣ 865
Opener	Overcaller	Responder	Advancer
1NT	2♣	2♦	pass
2♥	pass	2NT	pass
?			

? is for Opener

5.

♠ A87	♥ KQ8	♦ 96	♣ AJ53
Opener	Overcaller	Responder	Advancer
1NT	2♦	2♠	pass
3♣	pass	?	

6.

♠ 8	♥ AJ8	♦ QJ974	♣ A986
Opener	Overcaller	Responder	Advancer
1NT	2♠	dbl	pass
3♦	pass	?	

4.

Answers to Exercise on Priority #3

1. 3NT, scrambling
2. Four hearts, two spade losers
3. Pass, minimum and no Stopper
4. 4 hearts, maximum
5. Three notrump, Scrambling
6. Five diamonds

CHAPTER IV

Priority #4

Minor Suits

Notrump interference raises new challenges in our quest to reach the proper level when our hands are unsuitable for notrump play and we do not have a Major suit fit. In order to counter that problem and to assure that the contract is played by the stronger hand, we will employ the following bids:

1. **3♥** at least 5/5 in both Majors, Game force
2. **3♠** transfer **to 4♣.**
3. **4♣** *Game forcing* transfer **to 4♦**
4. **4♦** transfer to **4♥**
5. **4♥** transfer to **4♠**
6. **4♠** Quantitative Invitation to 6NT
7. **4NT** Blackwood or RKC Blackwood
8. **5♣** over a Major, 5/5 in the Minors

These bids are applicable directly after the overcall **and** during the course of the bidding, **when it is obvious that these bids could not be natural. We do not play Gerber in SONTI**.

When Responder's initial or subsequent bid is 3♠, he has a distributional hand and **does not** want to play in notrump. With a long club suit (at least six) that you would like to play in a club part score, **start with 2♠**. If partner bids 3♣, pass. *However, if Opener bids 2NT, you cannot bid 3♣ "to play" because that sequence is Stayman or Puppet Stayman.* You could pass 2NT, but if you want to play in clubs, you now must bid 3♠ which is a transfer to 4♣. This sequence is not forward going. It is simply the way that Responder, who was gambling that you would bid 3♣ so that you could play there, bails out. You should be cautious before bidding 2♠ to transfer to 3♣ with the intention of playing there, since you could end up playing in 4♣.

Remember, you don't have to "rescue" partner from playing in 1NT after an overcall. "Pass" is often be the best course of action.

When you have a hand that is unsuitable for notrump and would like to invite or drive to **Game or Slam** in clubs, bid 3♠ to transfer to clubs. In response to Responder's 3♠, **when Opener has a Minimum, he shows it by bidding 3NT.** After this discouraging bid, Responder can sign off at 4♣, bid 5♣ or explore for slam. If Opener has a Maximum, in response to 3♠, he makes the encouraging bid of **4♣**, which makes him the Declarer, sets clubs as the trump suit and prepares the four-level for control bids and/or 4NT if Responder wants to explore for a Slam.

Unless the overcall is 2♠, with a long diamond suit (at least six) that you would like to play in a diamond part score, bid 3♦, and partner will pass. After a spade overcall, a 3♦ bid would be a transfer to hearts, so if you want to play in a diamond part score, you will have to bid **4♣** to transfer to diamonds and then pass 4♦. If the overcall is 2♣, you could double and pass the 2♦ response, but bidding 3♦ directly with a long suit is often better because it will be preemptive.

If your hand is unsuitable for notrump and you want to play in 5♦ or invite slam in diamonds, bid 4♣ directly to transfer to diamonds. When Opener completes the transfer by bidding 4♦, diamonds becomes the agreed trump suit, with the strong hand being the Declarer, and the four level can be used for Control bids and/or 4NT to explore for slam.

Except when 2♠ is the overcall, and Responder wants to stop in diamond part score but can't bid 3♦ because that would have been a heart transfer, **the 4♣ bid is forcing to 5♦ since Responder could have bid 3♦ directly to play in a diamond part score.**

038.   ♠ 8   ♥ 8   ♦ J9   ♣ AJ1087654

After any overcall except clubs, bid 2♠. If partner bids 3♣, pass. If partner bids 2NT, 3♦ or 3♥, bid 3♠ which is a transfer to 4♣ which you will pass. *If partner bids 3♠ over your 2♠, bid 3NT and partner will bid 4♣ which you will pass.* 3NT is the "scrambling 3NT" and cannot be natural because both your 2♠ and Opener's 3♠ denied a stopper.

The 3S bid by Responder is always a transfer to clubs, whether it is bid directly after the overcall or indirectly as shown in the above example.

039.   ♠ 10   ♥8   ♦ KQ109853   ♣ 654

After any overcall except diamonds bid 3♦.   Note the difference between this hand and the previous one. We do not bid 2♠ first when we have a long diamond suit and less than invitational values.

040.   ♠ AQ   ♥ 87   ♦ KQJ10432   ♣ K8

After any overcall except diamonds, bid 4♣ which is a transfer to diamonds, **forcing to Game** and sets diamonds as the trump suit. **(4♣ is not Gerber in SONTI).**   After the 4♦ response make a cue bid of 4♠ and partner will take control from there.

He will know that you have slam aspirations because you didn't bid 5♦. He will also know that you have a control in spades and none in hearts (because you bypassed it). If he has a Minimum, he might bid 5♦ and you should pass. If he wants more information, he can bid 4NT or make a cue bid of 5♣ if he has the ace of clubs.

041.   ♠8   ♥ K5   ♦ AQJ10974   ♣ Q98

After any overcall except diamonds, bid 4♣ to transfer to 4♦ and raise to 5♦.

042.   ♠ 98   ♥5   ♦AJ6   ♣ KQ98653

After any overcall except clubs, start with 3♠. If Opener bids 3NT indicating a Minimum, bid 4♣ which is "to play" but if he bids 4♣, bid 5♣

.

Exercise on Priority #4

1.
♠ K87	♥ 85	♦ A2	♣ AKQ1075
Opener	Overcaller	Responder	Advancer
1NT	2♥	2♠	pass
3♠	pass	?	

2.
♠ A8	♥ K5	♦ 2	♣ KQ9875
Opener	Overcaller	Responder	Advancer
1NT	2♦	3♠	pass
4♣	pass	?	

3.
♠ J5	♥ 6	♦ QJ109864	♣ J75
Opener	Overcaller	Responder	Advancer
1NT	2♥	?	

4.
♠9	♥65	♦ 984	♣KQJ7542
Opener	Overcaller	Responder	Advancer
1NT	2♥	2♠	pass
3♦	pass	?	

5.
♠74	♥ A93	♦ KQJ1043	♣ A3
Opener	Overcaller	Responder	Advancer
1NT	2♠	4♣	pass
4♦	pass	?	

6.
♠ J7	♥ KQ3	♦ QJ10432	♣ A8
Opener	Overcaller	Responder	Advancer
1NT	2♠	?	

7.	♠ J7	♥ Q108	♦ KQ10432	♣ 93
	Opener	Overcaller	Responder	Advancer
	1NT	2♣	dbl	pass
	2♦	pass	?	

8.	♠ 9	♥ 86	♦ QJ108432	♣ Q65
	Opener	Overcaller	Responder	Advancer
	1NT	2♥	?	

9.	♠ 9	♥ KQ8	♦ A97	♣ AQJ654
	Opener	Overcaller	Responder	Advancer
	1NT	2♠	3♠	pass
	4♣	pass	?	

Answers to Exercise on Priority #4

1. Four spades, two heart losers, no slam
2. Five clubs, Opener has a Maximum
3. Three diamonds
4. Three spades, transfer to clubs
5. Four hearts, cue bid
6. Double
7. Three diamonds, invitation to 3NT with fitting honor,
8. Three diamonds
9. Four diamonds, cue bid

5

The Michaels Cue Bid

The Michaels Cue Bid is an overcaller's cue bid in opponent's Opening bid suit. It denotes a two-suited hand containing at least five cards in each suit. When Opener's suit is a Minor, the cue bid denotes at least five cards in both Majors. The partner of the cue bidder (unless the Responder bids) is forced to bid and usually bids the Major he prefers.

When the Opener's suit is a Major, a cue bid of that suit denotes at least five cards in the other Major and at least five cards in an unspecified Minor. When Advancer has at least three cards in the "other" Major, he normally usually bids that suit. When he does not, he can discover which Minor suit his partner has by bidding 2NT.

SONTI is compatible **and logical** with the Michaels Cue Bid because, after partner's opening bid of 1NT and a natural suit overcall, there are still three remaining unbid suits, similarly to the previous Michaels scenario.

In SONTI when the overcall is in a Major, the cue bid of that suit similarly denotes at least five cards in the other Major and five cards in an unspecified Minor suit. With at least 3-card support for the other Major, Opener bids that Major and Responder will decide whether to pass, raise to Game or look for a Slam. With less than three card support for the other Major, however, Opener cannot bid 3NT to identify the Minor

because that bid would be natural. If the preponderance of Opener's high card strength is in the overcalled suit and he has "coverage" for both Minors, or the one he suspects his partner doesn't have, he may want to play in 3NT despite the unbalanced nature of Responder's hand. However, it is usually not a good idea to play in 3NT when partner has 5/5 or 5/6 distribution. Therefore, when Opener has only 2-card support for the Major he may bid three or four of the "other Major" (depending upon whether he has a Minimum or Maximum) even though he likely has only a seven card fit (partner could have had 6/5 distribution, but even then he would have to hope the six card suit was the Major, not the Minor. If Opener is short in the Majors and long in the Minors, he can identify Responder's 5-card Minor suit by bidding 4♣ to play in Responder's long Minor suit.

When the overcall is a natural 2♦, there should be no ambiguity if Responder bids 3♦, as a cue bid, even though 3♦ in SONTI usually conventionally denotes a long diamond suit and a weak hand. The Responder would not want to play in diamonds when Overcaller has at least five cards in that suit. Therefore, a cue bid of the diamond overcall will denote at least five cards in both Majors and be invitational.

If the overcall is 2♣ and you are playing SONTI over 2♣, you cannot make a Michaels Cue Bid of 3♣, because that bid would be Stayman or Puppet Stayman. In order to show the **invitational** hand with at least five cards in the majors after a club overcall when playing SONTI over 2♣, we make a transfer or translay to spades and follow by bidding hearts. That sequence denotes 5/4 in the Majors, but if partner bids 3NT, you can bid hearts a second time to confirm that you have five.

On the other hand, if you and partner decide not to play SONTI over a 2♣ overcall, a double of 2♣ can be played as a stolen bid implementing Stayman, thereby making 3♣ available for the Michaels Cue Bid showing both Major Suits with an invitational hand. **In SONTI, we play that the bid of 3♥ denotes a Game forcing hand with at least five cards in both Major suits.**

Chapter V

Overcalls at the Three Level

Our responses after a 3-level overcall are somewhat similar to those at the 2-level but there are several exceptions.

1. The forcing 2♠ bid becomes the forcing 3♠ bid, denying a Stopper **or** showing a distributional hand that is unsuitable for no trump. It is not a transfer to clubs. Opener bids 3NT with a Stopper and 4♣ without one, which responder can pass or raise if he has a long club suit. Otherwise Responder and opener proceed to bid "up the line". When opener has no stopper and a good 5-card Major, he bids four of that suit.

2. Double is not penalty. It is similar to the translay double at the two level.

3. Responder's bids of 3♦ or 3♥ are Transfers and the bid of 3♠ or double of 3♠ can also be utilized as a transfer to 4♣ by a pass of that bid.

4. All 4-level bids are transfers, except 4♠ which is a quantitative invitation to 6NT, and 4NT which is Blackwood or RKC Blackwood.

5. We do not use Stayman or Puppet Stayman.

6. With a "good" invitational hand or better and a Stopper, bid 3NT.

043. ♠ AQJ866   ♥8   ♦ 95   ♣ KJ7

Over any 3-level overcall except spades, make a Texas Transfer bid of 4♥ to transfer to 4♠ and pass.

044.   ♠ K76   ♥ QJ5   ♦ 9   ♣ AQ8542

Over, 3♥ or 3♠, bid 3NT. **Over 3♦,** start with 3♠ and pass 3NT, 4♥ or 4♠ After 4♣ bid 5♣.

045.   ♠ AQJ106   ♥ J5   ♦ 93   ♣ A542

Over 3♣ or **3♦,** bid 3♥ and after partner bids 3S, bid 4. After 3H, double (stolen bid) to transfer to 3S and then bid 4S.

046.   ♠ J   ♥ 65   ♦ AKJ9874   ♣ K94

After any 3-level overcall except diamonds, bid 4♣ to transfer to 4♦ and raise to 5.

047.   ♠ 97   ♥ 9   ♦863   ♣AQ98542

After any 3-level overcall, bid 3♠. If partner bids 4♣, pass. If he bids 3NT, bid 4♣. **This bid is not Gerber or Stayman.** It is "to play" and partner will pass.

Exercise on Three Level Overcalls

1.   ♠ K87   ♥ 95   ♦ K974   ♣ AK96

Opener	Overcaller	Responder	Advancer
1NT	3♥	3♠	pass
4C	pass	4♦	pass
4♠	pass	?	

2.   ♠ 8   ♥ 5   ♦ KQJ8642   ♣ J643

Opener	Overcaller	Responder	Advancer
1NT	3♥	?	pass

3.   ♠ KQ876   ♥ 75   ♦ K97   ♣ A96

Opener	Overcaller	Responder	Advancer
1NT	3♣	3♥	pass
3♠	pass	?	

4.   ♠ 87   ♥ A542   ♦ KQ6   ♣ J643

Opener	Overcaller	Responder	Advancer
1NT	3♠	dbl	pass
4♣	pass	?	

5.   ♠ K864   ♥ 7   ♦ AQ86   ♣ QJ75

Opener	Overcaller	Responder	Advancer
1NT	3♥	3♠	pass
4♣	pass	4♦	pass
4 NT	pass	?	

Answers to Exercise on 3-level overcalls

1. Pass   2. Four clubs, transfer   3. Three notrump
4. Four hearts   5. Five clubs, 4 NT is "Scrambling"

CHAPTER VI

Conventional Overcalls

Many conventions have been developed for overcalls of 1NT. So far, we have only discussed overcalls after natural suits at the two and three level. We will now focus on responses after conventional overcalls. We will categorize them by the meaning of their initial bid, rather than listing the numerous conventions, since it is after the first call that you need to take action or pass.

Overcall is a Penalty Double

A penalty double of one notrump is not a convention but is generally used to describe a hand of at least equal value to that of the Opener. With a balanced hand and four to six high card points, Responder should be content to pass and expect partner to make 1NT or be down one or two. With a 5-card or longer suit, he should consider bidding that suit. **The fewer high card points he has, the more he should favor playing in his long suit** since partner will be challenged to find entries to his hand. With a flat hand and 7 or more high card points, a redouble should be considered.

048.   ♠ J6   ♥ Q9865   ♦9   ♣ J752

The overcall is a penalty double. Rescue partner by bidding 2♥.

049.   ♠ K76   ♥ Q106   ♦Q65   ♣ J1052

After a penalty double, redouble.

6.

Overcall is an Artificial Bid Showing A Long Suit

Non-Penalty doubles after a 1NT opening are sometimes a double which is a relay to 2♣ and indicates a suit of at least six-cards. After the relay, doubler will bid his long suit or pass, if his long suit is clubs. The procedure **for Responder** after this conventional double is different than after a penalty double. In the latter case, you are looking to "protect" Opener since the doubler is sitting behind him with a hand of equal or greater value. It is rare that advancer will pass this artificial double. Therefore, with limited values you can pass and await advancer's bid before taking any action.

Vulnerability is important as you may fare better by doubling and setting your opponent rather than making a part-score contract. Another reason to pass is to discover which suit will likely be led and to assess your prospects of success against that lead. If you pass, you will discover the 'danger" suit" and be able to use all of the tools you have learned in the preceding pages. On the other hand, it may be better to ignore the double and preempt your opponent's interference when you have values that would produce a playable contract, especially if you might be able to make Game. Another option is to redouble. With a distributional hand this may be ill advised, but with a balanced hand of seven high card points or more, a redouble could be quite profitable, especially if your opponents are vulnerable and you are not.

050.   ♠ 853   ♥ K8   ♦ K987   ♣ Q987

The overcall is a double showing a long suit.

62

Redouble. You can't be sure which suit will be bid and your prospects for Game are remote. A redouble should be successful.

Overcall is an Artificial Bid Showing Two Suits

Some conventions deploy an artificial bid to designate a hand with **two long suits**. With a balanced hand and seven or eight high card points you should consider a double. Your odds of making Game are low and the odds of opponents going down in any suit at the two level are high. With a balanced hand and nine high card points or more, you will have to decide whether to pursue a penalty double or explore for Game. Vulnerability will be an important factor in your decision along with your prospects for Game.

If you have just nine high card points and vulnerability is favorable, a penalty double will frequently be a better choice. When your hand is unbalanced, however, you may be able to make Game with fewer than nine high card points and your opponents are more likely to make their contract at the two level. In that case you should bid constructively. After determining the identity of the two suits, with nine or more high card points, proceed with the assumption that you do not want to play in either one. Therefore, a bid by you or partner in either suit is artificial. If the **two suits are hearts and spades**, and the artificial overcall is "double", 2♣, or 2♦, **use the principle utilized in showing control bids by bidding your Stoppers "up the line".** Therefore, you will bid 2♥ to show a heart Stopper but no spade Stopper, 2♠ to show a spade Stopper and no heart Stopper and 2NT or 3NT to show Stoppers in both Majors. After your call, when Opener discovers that both suits can be stopped, he bids 2NT with a Minimum or 3NT with a Maximum. If Opener rebids 2NT and you have more than invitational values, bid 3NT. After entering the bidding and discovering that at least one suit is not stopped, your only options are the other two suits. At that point, you bid "up the line" starting with the lowest of those suits in which you have four cards.

051.　　　　♠ KJ5　　♥ 8　　♦ K9875　　♣ A86

The overcall is 2♦ showing at least five cards in both Majors. The first priority when there are two known suits is to show a Stopper "up the line" in one of those suits. On the above hand, bid 2♠ to show your spade Stopper. This is not the forcing 2♠ bid. Partner will know you don't have a heart Stopper and, if he has one, he will bid 2NT or 3NT. If he does not have a heart Stopper, he will start an up the line sequence. **It's not a very long line!** He can't bid notrump because there is no heart Stopper and you don't want to play in hearts or spades. That leaves only clubs and diamonds. Following the "up the line" procedure on the above hand, Opener will start with his lowest 4-card suit. If he bids 3♣, bid 3♦ and with a Minimum and less than four diamonds, he will pass, but if he raises to four, bid 5♦. If partner bids 3♦ over your 2♠, you should also bid 5♦. Your spades are favorably placed and partner does not have the ace or king of hearts. Consequently, all of your high card points will be "working".

Overcall is the Unusual Notrump

The overcall of 2NT is called the unusual notrump. While it is commonly used after an opening bid of one of a suit, it can also be used as the overcall of the opening of 1NT. The bid describes a hand with five or more cards in both Minor suits. After the Unusual Notrump overcall, when we have sufficient

64

values and a five card Major, we bid 3♦ to transfer to hearts or 3♥ to transfer to spades. When we have a 4-card Major, we bid 3♣, which is Stayman or Puppet Stayman. In this way, we have the best chance of finding a Major suit fit. After our Stayman bid, Opener can bid 3NT if he has Stoppers in both Minor suits. When Responder has length or strength in the Minors but not the Majors, he should consider a penalty double. Of course, opponents are going to "run" to a Minor suit, but now either you or Opener can double again for penalty. After Responder's 3♣ Stayman call, if opponents want to play in clubs, they will have to do so at the four level, which is not likely. Advancer may bid 3♦, but both you are partner will still have options.

052.　　　♠ KJ53　　♥ QJ8　　♦ 86　　♣ A875

Over 2NT showing both Minors, bid 3♣ which is Stayman. If Opener bids 3♠, raise to 4 and if you are playing Puppet Stayman and he bids 3♥, raise to four. If he bids 3NT, you will pass and assume he has a diamond Stopper. If **Advancer** bids 3♦ over your 3♣ and partner passes, you should **double**. If partner had a Major suit, he would have bid it and if he had Stoppers in both Minors, he would have bid 3NT, so Game is unlikely.

Overcall is a Natural Bid Showing Two Suits

Some two-suited conventional overcalls begin with a natural bid of two of a suit. Unless the overcall is 2♥ showing hearts and spades, you won't know what the second suit is. The procedure in this situation is quite direct. We temporarily ignore the second suit which is unknown and concentrate on discovering whether we have a Stopper in the first suit. Therefore, **all our bids are identical to those employed after natural one-suited overcalls.** Especially effective will be the forcing 2♠ bid. In addition to the customary benefits of denying a Stopper and setting up the opportunity for Opener to

6

further describe his hand, this bid may prevent opponents from introducing their second suit at the two level. If they do bid their second suit, whether at the two or three level, we continue to apply the same set of responses to that suit.

053.　　　♠ 963　♥ KJ75　♦ A83　♣ K84

Overcall is 2♣ showing clubs and a higher suit. Disregarding the unknown second suit, bid 3♣, which is Stayman or Puppet. This will probably prevent opponents from introducing their second suit as they may be reluctant to enter the bidding at the three level. At the same time, we have the opportunity to find a 4/4 or 5/3 fit in a Major suit, in which case having a Stopper in either suit is irrelevant. Some conventions call for bidding the Major suit at the two level first and then the Minor at the 3-level, such as the next hand.

054.　　　♠ J63　♥KJ75　♦J83　♣ AK8

Overcall is 2S showing spades and a Minor. Double to enable the Forcing 2♠ bid and proceed as you would if there were no second suit. If opponents bid their second suit at the 3-level and you or partner have a Stopper in spades and the second suit, you can carry on to 3NT or elect to double for penalty. Advancer can't have much and will be reluctant to bid at the three level. You may also be able to identify a heart fit, in which case having a Stopper would be irrelevant.

Overcall is 2D showing diamonds and a higher suit. Bid a forcing 2♠ which is likely opponent's second suit, thereby stealing what may be their best contract. If partner bids 2NT, bid 3♣ which is Stayman or Puppet. If you find an 8-card heart fit, bid 4♥. If not, bid 3NT. If partner does not have a diamond Stopper and bids 3♣, bid 3♥.

Exercise on Conventional Overcalls

. ♠ K8743	♥ J65	♦ QJ6	♣ Q9
* Diamonds & higher suit			
Opener	Overcaller	Responder	Advancer
1NT	2♦ *	2♥	pass
2♠	pass	?	

2. ♠ 8	♥ 5	♦ KQJ8642	♣ J643
* long suit, club relay			
Opener	Overcaller	Responder	Advancer
1NT	dbl*	?	

3. ♠ 876	♥ 753	♦ A97	♣ KJ
*long suit club relay			
Opener	Overcaller	Responder	Advancer
1NT	dbl*	?	

4. ♠ 9863	♥ QJ2	♦ QJ64	♣ K6
* hearts and spades			
Opener	Overcaller	Responder	Advancer
1NT	2♦*	2♥	pass
3♣	pass	?	

5. ♠ A97	♥ J65	♦ KJ	♣ 86
* clubs & higher suit			
Opener	Overcaller	Responder	Advancer
1NT	2♣ *	2♠	pass
2NT	pass	?	

6. ♠ K832	♥ KJ52	♦ QJ63	♣ 8
* Minors			
Opener	Overcaller	Responder	Advancer
1NT	2NT *	3♣	pass
3♥	pass	?	

Answers to Exercise on Conventional Overcalls

1. Two notrump, spades invitation
2. Four clubs, transfer
3. Redouble
4. Three diamonds
5. Pass
6. Four hearts

SUMMARY OF FEIT RESPONSES

The following is a list of the **initial bid by Responder and initial rebid by Opener** following an overcall of 1NT, in a natural suit at the 2-level.

Double of 2♣, 2♦ or 2♥:

Translay double.: Either a ("stolen bid") transfer or an indication that Responder has invitational values. Opener's mandatory response is to bid the next highest suit.

2♦ or 2♥:

Traditional Jacoby Transfer. Opener bids the next highest suit.

2♠:

Forcing 2♠ Bid. Shows no Stopper and asks Opener to further describe his hand. Additional function is to transfer to clubs. Opener responds, **in order of precedence**: 3♦, 3♥, or 3♠ with no Stopper and five cards in that suit; 2NT with a Stopper and a minimum or 3NT with a Stopper and a Maximum; 3♣ with no Stopper and no 5-card diamond, heart or spade suit

Double of 2♠:

Same as 2♠ above, (Stolen Bid). Opener's rebid is also the same as above.

2NT:

Invitational values with a Stopper. Opener passes with a Minimum, raises to 3NT with a Maximum and bids 3♥ or 3♠ with maximum and 5-card Major **which is forcing to Game**.

3♣:

Stayman or Puppet Stayman, by partnership agreement. **Guarantees a Stopper and is Forcing to Game or four of a Minor.** Over Stayman, Opener bids three of his Major if he has at least four and 3♦ if he has no 4-card Major. Playing Puppet Stayman, Opener bids three of his Major if he has five, 3♦ if he has one or both 4-card majors, and 3NT with no four or 5-card Major.

3♦:

Over 2♣ or 2♥, shows at least 6 diamonds and less than invitational values. Opener passes.

Over **2♦**, shows at least five cards in both Majors with invitational values. With a Minimum Opener bids 3♥ or 3♠ (longer suit) and with a Maximum, bids 4♥ or 4♠.

Over 2♠, 3♦ is a transfer to hearts. With insufficient values for Game, if Responder wants to play in a diamond part-score, he must bid **4♣** to transfer to **4♦** and then pass.

3♥:

At least five cards in both Majors and forcing to Game.
Opener bids 4♥ or corrects to **4♠**

3♠:

Transfer to 4♣. Opener bids 3NT with a Minimum and 4♣ with a Maximum. Responder corrects 3NT to clubs at the proper level.

3NT:

Game going values with a Stopper.

4♣:

Transfer to diamonds. **Game forcing**. Opener bids 4♦.

4♦:

Transfer to 4♥. Opener bids 4♥.

4♥:

Transfer to 4♠. Opener bids 4♠
.

4♠:

Quantitative invitation to 6NT. Opener bids 4NT with minimum and 6NT with maximum.

4NT:

Blackwood or RKC Blackwood. Opener shows number of aces or key cards

5C: Over Major

Responder has at least five cards in both Minors. Opener chooses to pass 5♣ or bid.

Comparison of SONTI with Lebensohl

Advantages of Lebensohl Over SONTI

In my opinion, there is only one advantage of Lebensohl over SONTI and that one is arguable. Playing Lebensohl, the double of the overcall of your partner's 1NT opening bid is for penalty. Yes, there are hands where you will be sitting with a stack behind Overcaller and can punish him or her severely by doubling, especially when there is no place to run. However, just setting them doubled may not be the best result. For example, if you are vulnerable and they are not and you can make Game, you will have to set them 4 tricks to make a profit. That could be problematic, especially if they find a good fit. When the opponents are vulnerable, it is certainly more tempting to double them, but it may be more difficult to set them because it is likely that good opponents will have a much stronger and/or distributional hand to come in vulnerable over your partner's 1NT opening. If you are doubling a 2-level Major suit contract and they make it, you will be doubling them into Game. Playing SONTI, it is not possible for Responder to double the overcall directly for penalty, nor is it possible for Opener to convert a double by Responder to a penalty double by passing, as he or she is obliged to bid (unless RHO bids). On the other hand, after doubling, **Responder is guaranteed to get another bid** and, when the opponents reenter the bidding, **a second double by Responder is for penalty and can be passed by Opener.**

Fifteen Advantages of SONTI Over Lebensohl

1. In Lebensohl, the signature bid by Responder after the overcall is 2NT, which starts a relay to 3 clubs. **The partnership cannot play in 2NT even though it may be their best contract!** Neither the 2NT or 3♣ transfer describes the Opener's or Responder's hand. These bids are simply a mechanism to set up further bids. The opponents have already robbed you of bidding space with their overcall, and the 2NT/3♣ sequence is simply adding insult to injury. Conversely in SONTI, the unique new bids conserve bidding space, allowing for the transfer of vital information at a lower level.

2. In SONTI, a direct bid of 2NT over opponent's overcall **is natural.** It shows invitational values for Game and a Stopper in Opponent's suit. This is **logical** and consistent with normal bidding practice, wherein bidding notrump, after opponents have bid a suit, indicates a Stopper **in that suit.**

3. In Lebensohl, a direct bid of 3NT by Responder shows values for Game but no Stopper in the opponent's suit. This is **illogical** and difficult to grasp and remember! In SONTI, the bid of 3NT after the overcall is **natural and logical**. It shows a hand with values for Game and a Stopper.

4. In Lebensohl, when neither partner has a Stopper, it is often necessary to scramble for a playable contract at the four level. In SONTI, we will know sooner and will usually be able to search for and find a playable contract at the three level.

5. The Lebensohl convention **does not utilize transfers**. If Responder has a long Major suit and limited values, he bids the suit at the two level. Opener must pass and the hand will be played from the **"wrong side"**. This is a **serious failing** of Lebensohl as the success of many contracts is frequently dependent upon whether the player with the stronger hand is able to play the hand. In SONTI we **use transfers to all suits** to assure that the Opener, with the stronger hand is the Declarer.

6. In Lebensohl, the bid of three of a Major suit is Game forcing. **There is no direct invitational bid.** Responder can start with 2NT and then bid his Major after the relay to show his 5-card suit and an invitational hand but this sequence is problematic. It is only to be used when Responder's suit is higher than that of the Overcaller. This is one of the hard to remember aspects of Lebensohl. In SONTI, we use transfers to a Major at the two level, which **facilitates invitational raises, similarly to when there is no overcall**.

7. In addition to transfers, another important bid which is not utilized in Lebensohl is **"Stolen Bids"**. This popular and useful bid is compatible with SONTI and is extremely valuable as it **takes up no bidding space**.

8. When neither partner has a Stopper, it is imperative to try to find a fit in a Major suit. Lebensohl employs a cue bid for this purpose which is **illogical** and **will frequently force the bidding to the 4-level** when a fit is not found. In SONTI we use the Stayman Convention to find a Major suit fit, which is easier to remember, more effective and **logical.** Puppet Stayman can also be used (and is

recommended) in SONTI if you and partner are comfortable playing that Convention.

9. Only in SONTI is **Opener** able to show a 5-card Major suit at the three level, which can be vital to finding a 5/3 fit in a Major, (played by the Opener).

10. Only in SONTI is **Opener** able to show five diamonds, at the 3-level which can be vital to finding a Part-score, Game or Slam in diamonds, especially when no Stopper exists and notrump is not a viable option

11. SONTI includes new bids that facilitate the bidding of Game and Slam in the Minor Suits.

12. Only in SONTI are both Opener and Responder able to show a Partial Stopper at the 3-level, facilitating the ability to reach a successful 3NT contract when neither one has a full stopper.

13. Only in SONTI do we have a bid to invite Game in a Major suit, while simultaneously specifying whether we have a Stopper.

14. Only in SONTI can we utilize the Michaels Cue Bid to describe a two-suited hand.

15. **SONTI is more functional, more logical, easier to learn and easier to use than Lebensohl.**

Made in the USA
Lexington, KY
15 December 2019